Answered Prayer is God's Will for You

Ian Christensen

D1301623

New Wine Press

New Wine Press
P.O. Box 17
Chichester
England PO20 6YB

Scripture quotations are from:

AV Authorised Version
RSV Revised Standard Version
Copyright © 1962. Harper & Row, New York.
NIV New International Version
Copyright © 1973, 1978 International Bible Society,
published by Hodder & Stoughton.

ISBN: 0 947852 90 5

Typeset by CRB Typesetting Services, Ely, Cambs.
Printed by Clays Ltd, Bungay, Suffolk.

Contents

Acknowledgements

To all those who gave of their time and effort to assist with the various aspects of the manuscript. In particular Shona Fraser, Peter Cornish and Andrew.

To my lovely wife Dennise who has encouraged and prayed for me throughout the project and assisted me with the typing. Also to my three precious children Angela, John and Sarah for sacrificially releasing me to write this book.

Finally, to all the members of the New Life Christian Centre, Wembley who have prayed and supported me all along the way.

Foreword

This book is a prescription for the condition of prayerlessness. It is a thought provoking, and challenging pursuit of a subject that is central to our Christian faith.

Individual believers, as well as congregations, are being called today to pray more. It is God's way in this last decade of the century to prepare us for a spiritual awakening.

Prayer is not a natural function, but a spiritual one. It requires us saying 'no' to the flesh and 'yes' to the Spirit. Jesus said to his disciples, *'The spirit is willing, but the body is weak.'* (Matt 26:41) He said this to disciples who went to sleep when they prayed!

To those who find they are too busy to pray remember Jesus' words to Martha: *'"Martha, Martha," the Lord answered, "you are worried and upset about many things, but only one thing is needed. Mary has chosen what is better, and it will not be taken away from her."'* (Luke 10:41) God has inspired Ian Christensen to write a book that will help you to see that prayer is a central need in your life, and that you must keep choosing it.

I am sure that this book will inspire you to make prayer central in your personal life, in your family and in your church.

Jean Darnall

Foreword

No-one is such an expert in the art of prayer that he/she outgrows the need to learn more. We never graduate. The secret power of prayer remains unexplored territory for many Christians. Yet it is as simple as a child having a heart to heart talk with his/her father. God does hear. He definitely cares and what is more He answers. Implicit trust in God never goes unrewarded. It must however be said that God does not always meet our expectations. He does not always answer our prayers in the way and the time we want. His timetable is often different. It is His prerogative to exercise His Sovereign will and wisdom in His dealings with us. He always answers but He can and does say *yes*, *no* or *wait*. Personally I do not feel good when He says *no* or *wait*. I always want Him to say 'Yes'. What is more I always want Him to do it *now* and exactly the way I thought it out. I am learning that God does not love me less when He does things differently to my own expectations but to the contrary. He has my best interest at heart and does only those things which are for my ultimate good. I must confess I do not understand it sometimes but I rest in His love.

The existence and threat of demonic powers and activities against the people is real not imagined. Christians need to learn a whole lot more how to stand up and resist the enemy attacks on our lives, jobs, our children. If the people of God will be a force to be reckoned with in our generation, if we will be instruments for change in our community and if we will be the prophetic Kingdom people then we must talk less and rediscover the power of intercession and spiritual warfare.

I have known Ian, his family and church for five years during which time I have grown to respect his burden and also practice of prayer. Here is a man who actually prays. The thoughts expressed here come out of his own experience and walk with the Lord.

I commend this book with the hope that in the reading of it many more hearts will be challenged and stirred to pray more effectively. More things are wrought through prayer than we can properly assess or imagine.

Philip Mohabir

Preface

The scenery was breath-taking; all around me were picturesque hills and mountains. I was nine years old and I remembered vividly how I danced for joy, when I discovered my parents were sending me to boarding school at St Mary's High School up at the hill station of Mount Abu in India. I had heard that it was an excellent missionary school run by a religious community called the Irish Christian Brothers. Shortly after I arrived there I would often climb up a little mound beside the school and sit alone and cry. I wept and prayed to a God I did not really know at all.

I cried because I missed my parents so much, and I prayed because it seemed the right thing to do. I climbed the mound and sat in its hollow top to hide away from the other boys so that no one would see my tears.

From the top of the mound, I could see part of the eighteen mile long road that turned and twisted, hugging the side of the mountain as it gradually led the cars and buses up from the plain below. I never told anyone where I was going when I went up the mound, and when one of the boys enquired about my frequent disappearances, I easily dismissed his enquiry, as little boys often do.

I cried again and prayed as best I could. On this occasion, as I prayed my eyes observed afresh the beautiful scenery all around me. I also noticed a line of cars in the distance slowly making their way up the winding road from the plain below. I noticed a grey car among them, and forgetting for a moment that my parents were hundreds of miles away, I prayed with the tears still streaming down my face, 'Please God, let my dad be in that grey car.'

A few minutes later the grey car pulled up the steep drive to the school. I was not surprised at this, as there were nearly two hundred boys in the school and visitors came frequently. I peered over the top of the mound straining to see who was in the car. It was a man in a military uniform! Could it really be? – incredible! To my utter amazement it was my father, who was a lieutenant colonel in the army. I knew that my father did not like to see me cry, so I hastily wiped my face and ran excitedly down to meet him and fell joyfully into his strong arms.

I never really gave this incident much thought until some fifteen years later when I became a Christian. Whichever way I looked at this event, I came to the conclusion that God loved me and that He had revealed Himself to me that day. I did not know much about prayer then and it was to be many years later that I would discover – under the direction of my loving heavenly Father, that he desired to teach me how to pray and that the principles for answered prayer were clearly revealed in the Bible. The title of the book derives its inspiration from the words of Jesus: *'ask whatever you wish, and it will be given you'* (John 15:7 NIV).

In John 15:7, 8 (NIV) Jesus said *'If you remain in me and my words remain in you, ask whatever you wish, and it will be given you. This is to my Father's glory, that you bear much fruit, showing yourselves to be my disciples'.*

Although I shall always be learning about prayer, I have already experienced great joy in discovering that it is God's will to answer all our prayers. We simply need to learn to pray correctly, aligning our lives with His words. I humbly and sincerely pray that by the time you reach the end of this book you will believe and experience that *'answered prayer is God's will for you'*.

Chapter 1

Why is it so Important to Pray?

I collapsed exhausted into bed, it had been a busy day and my whole being was crying out for rest. As I began to slip into a restful sleep I was awakened by the sound of crying. It was my daughter, Angela, who was standing next to the bed. Still in a daze, I asked what the problem was. I had been awakened on several occasions in the preceding years, by our other two children but Angela had never given us a troubled night since she was six weeks old. Her head and stomach seemed to be on fire and she was semi-delirious. I took her back to her room and began to pray quietly so as not to wake my wife Dennise. I had seen God heal our children overnight on many occasions. As I prayed for Angela my tired mind and body encouraged me to keep the prayer short. 'Pray a quick prayer', I thought, just say 'in the name of Jesus be healed', and go back to bed. I had taught my children from their earliest years that God would heal them when they were sick. To them it was nothing unexpected for Dad to pray, and for God to heal. I did pray for Angela but despite the previous times when God had healed, my level of faith was a low ebb due to my tiredness and having so recently been woken up.

*'But you, dear friends, build yourselves up in your
most holy faith and pray in the Holy Spirit'*
(Jude 20 NIV)

I put Angela to bed and returned to my much needed
sleep. Faith believes God for the answer but it seemed I
knew Angela would call me again. I was in and out of
her room at least three or four times, each time I hoped
she would be healed and fall asleep. If I was honest I was
not praying in faith at all, I was just hoping that she
would be healed of this awful fever, and rise in the
morning completely well as had happened on previous
occasions.

About the third or fourth time I was in her room I
decided that this had gone far enough. 'Never mind your
sleep Ian, get down and pray properly', I told myself. I
put my hand on Angela's head. She seemed to have a
raging fever and was still semi-delirious. I began to pray.
Now I was praying earnestly. I prayed with my mind and
I prayed continuously in the prayer language which the
Holy Spirit had given me, and meditated on the promises of healing in the Bible. A long time went by, an
hour, possibly two, while I persisted in earnest prayer.
Soon a strong determination rose up in me – Angela will
be healed of this sickness tonight.

As the minutes ticked by my level of faith seemed to
rise higher and higher (Jude 20). I stood over Angela
again and rebuked the fever – commanding it to leave,
declaring healing over my child in the name of Jesus!
This time I returned to bed confident that God had
touched Angela. I knew she was healed. I slept a sweet
sound sleep for the rest of the night. Angela awoke the
next morning before I did and jumped up and down in

her room saying 'I'm healed, I'm healed'. She waited for me to wake to tell me the good news. 'Dad, I did not want to wake you, because I knew you would be tired', she said. We have a God who answers prayer. Sometimes we need to persevere until the answer comes.

God Works Through Our Prayers

John Wesley said, 'It seems God is limited by our prayer life – that he can do nothing for humanity unless someone asks him'. God is sovereign, He can do whatever He wishes, but He has chosen to work in response to the prayers of His people. John Wesley, after his conversion engaged in much prayer and fasting along with his brother, Charles, and George Whitefield. These men's lives and ministries radically affected their generation and have continued to affect generations since. Every great person of power in the Bible and in contemporary Christianity has been a person of prayer.

E.M. Bounds, in his many fine books, expounds that a prayerless life produces an ineffective and powerless Christian walk. Jesus said in Matt 26:41 *'Watch and pray so that you will not fall into temptation'*. Yes, prayer does strengthen us against temptation. That is one of the many benefits of prayer. If you are really a Christian, I believe that deep within you is a desire to pray. Your spirit is willing (Matt 26:41) but there are forces ranged against us, attempting to stop us praying. I will be returning to this subject later.

As I write this book, I have been pastoring a church for more than eleven years, and I have learnt as a minister that the enemy is always trying to destroy what is good in my life and ministry. However, as I engage in regular prayer and motivate others around me to do the same, I see God's Kingdom come and His will done in my life and the lives of those around me, whilst the enemy constantly knows defeat (Matt 6:10). I can confidently say that if I had not learnt to pray in the midst of life-crushing problems (2 Corinthians 1:8, 11) I would almost certainly be without my wife, family, church and ministry today. Whilst some of the problems we face are undoubtedly a direct result of our own shortcomings, we nevertheless need to know how to deal with the devil when he comes against us to kill to steal and to destroy (John 10:10).

You may say – 'Well, God worked in a sovereign way to pull you through these problems'. If that were true, what about all the Christians whose marriages are broken and those ministers who have lost their wives, families, churches and ministries – could God not have worked in a sovereign way in their lives too? To conclude that these defeats come only as a result of sin and disobedience is, I believe, not the whole story. Many disastrous situations could have been averted if Christians had learnt to engage in effective warring prayer. In our own church in Wembley in London, we have seen many wonderful victories of healing and restored lives, and situations changed as we have engaged in effective prayer warfare.

Our God-Given Authority

In 2 Corinthians 4:4 Satan is given the title *'The god of this age'*. Paul gave him this title even after the victory of Christ on the cross. Where did Satan get this title from?

We read in Genesis 1:26, 28 that Adam was given the

honour, under God, of having dominion on the earth. When Adam disobeyed God and His word and listened to Satan's words, he fell into a state of sin and Satan was able to move into a position that God never intended him to have. Satan got this title by snatching it from Adam. He most certainly did not take this title through any victory over God himself. He won it in an evil way from the apple of God's eye, man.

However, the New Testament is clear in showing us that Jesus Christ soundly defeated Satan and his cohorts by his life, death and resurrection. After we are born again we have a delegated authority from Jesus whereby we can constantly subdue the forces of evil when they come against God's will for our lives. We can even engage in intercessory prayer and break the devil's power over the lives of others, so that they are released to make their own response to God. Jesus said, *'I have given you authority to trample on snakes and scorpions, and to overcome **all** the power of the enemy;'* (Luke 10:19 NIV). In Matthew 28:18 Jesus clearly states, *'All authority in heaven and on earth has been given to me.'* He goes on to tell his disciples to go out in this authority, given to them, to do the work they were called to do.

We must be Guided by God's Word

We discover God's general will for our lives by reading and meditating on God's words revealed in the Bible. Every Christian needs to engage in regular Bible study, at some level, to understand the various aspects of God's will for his or her life (Matth 4:4). A mind renewed by God's words (Romans 12:2) will be able to recognise the prompting of the Holy Spirit. We must be directed by both God's words and His Spirit to be strong and balanced Christians.

As part of God's Church which is both a family and an army, we have been given authority, under God, to subdue the enemy and bring about God's purposes on the earth. We are part of the eternal family of God under our heavenly father, through the blood of Jesus which binds us together as one. As God's army we are called to fight and subdue our common enemy, Satan, by the power of God's Holy Spirit. It is by prayer – **effective, persevering and enlightened** prayer – that we see God's kingdom come and His will being done on the earth. Matthew 6:9–10 (NIV):

> *'This is how you should pray:*
> *"Our Father in heaven,*
> *hallowed be your name,*
> *your kingdom come,*
> *your will be done*
> *on earth as it is in heaven."'*

Paul states in Romans 14:17 that the kingdom of God consists of righteousness, and peace and joy in the Holy Spirit. This dimension of kingdom life, Jesus tells us, is released as we pray – *'Your kingdom come your will be done'*. This is another good reason for prayer, perhaps one of the main reasons, but there are many more.

We need to understand the different kinds of prayer, for example intercessory prayer and 'The Prayer of Faith'. We need to understand how fasting can increase the effectiveness of our prayer. We need to understand why we need to pray. We can **Learn How To Pray** (Luke 11:1). God does not have any favourite children. All his promises as revealed in the Bible, are for every true believer who is now in covenant with God through the blood of Jesus Christ (Luke 22:20; 2 Peter 1:3, 4). These are some of the issues that I will deal with later in this book.

Imperfect, but Right with God

The life of David greatly encourages me. David made some very serious mistakes during his life. How would you like to have your major mistakes written in a book for anyone to read? I would not be very keen. If I wrote the book myself I could show myself in a pleasant light, but when the writers of Scripture just bluntly put down the facts as they were – poor David! Yet David is the only person in the whole Bible of whom it is written that he was a man after God's own heart. I can identify with David, he had wonderful victories, there were times of tremendous spirituality in his life and yet, there were times when David sinned, falling short of his high calling. Yet, in spite of all his human frailties and failures he consummated the work that Moses initiated. On more than one occasion it is recorded that David's heart smote him (1 Samuel 24:5; 2 Samuel 24:10), but through it all he got right with God again. He did not continue in rebellion and sin. We cannot justify any of David's sin, God did not. He dealt with David as a son, correcting and chastising him (Hebrews 12:3, 11).

I thank God that because of the blood of Jesus, we can confess our sin and forsake it, know that we are forgiven and move on with God as David did.

God has made a way for us under the New Covenant to stay in constant relationship and fellowship with Himself because of what Jesus has done for us. We can find

Healing, Wholeness and **Deliverance** from all the works of the devil wherever they are found (1 John 3:8). We can keep our hearts right with God and enjoy a successful prayer life free from guilt and condemnation (Romans 8:1, 2).

God Brings us Through the Difficult Times

I have known barren times earlier on in my ministry, when it seemed that all my prayers were simply bouncing off the ceiling. God seemed far away and everything seemed to be going wrong. Have you ever been through periods where everything seemed to be going wrong and you have thought that it could not possibly get worse, and then suddenly it got worse again and then again and yet again? I know something of how Job felt.

Job did not understand all that was happening to him but I thank God, that after a comparatively short period of intense suffering, Job was healed and blessed for one hundred and forty years (Job 42:16, 17). After praying for his friends and keeping his heart right, Satan's attacks were stopped by God and Job ended up as God really wanted, much wiser, stronger and doubly blessed in every way. If we are to draw conclusions from the beginning and the middle of the book of Job for today, surely we must not overlook the end of the book (Job 42:10, 17).

I thank God that he always brings us through the difficult patches into times of joy and blessing as we simply trust Him (2 Corinthians 1:9–11).

I have felt that I too have been through intense times of insecurity and suffering like Job. It was only as I began to learn to pray, that I found strength and revelation from God to climb out of these periods. One day this scripture came alive to me *'Is any one among you suffering? Let him pray.'* (James 5:13). Yes, answered prayer is wonderful, it brings joy (John 15:7–11).

The Lord corrected me and dealt with me during these periods and I learnt a number of things along the way. However, I humbly submit that I now enjoy answers to my prayers regularly. Not simply because I am living a better life than before, but because I have learnt where I was wrong in my prayer life.

Develop Your Own Faith

We could for convenience divide Scripture into two main categories – 1.) God's Commands and 2.) God's promises. The Lord's blessings are always poured out upon those who obey him (Deut 28:1, 2). All God's promises are appropriated by faith by his children which frequently happens through the medium of prayer.

If you pray for another Christian, their will is involved. You need to know what they believe and what they will do after you have prayed for them. Without proper instruction some answers to prayer can be lost. For instance when Jesus said in Mark 11:23 (NIV) *'I tell you the truth, if anyone says to this mountain, "Go throw yourself into the sea," and does not doubt in his heart but believes that what he says will happen, it will be done for him'*. There are certain conditions to this promise:

a) The person must not doubt in his heart

b) The person must believe that what he says will happen.

Then God will do it for him.

I can claim this promise for myself and remove demonic and other obstacles from my life but if I come against an obstacle in your life at your request and you do not have a clear understanding of the principles of faith as taught by Jesus, it will not always automatically happen for you.

Learn to Pray Effectively

Jesus told his disciples a parable to show them that they should always pray and not give up (Luke 18:1). Have you, like me, on numerous occasions felt like giving up? We can learn how to pray. I want to encourage you. The mere fact that Jesus taught on prayer and faith, shows us that we can learn how to get it right. Keep your heart right with God, keep learning **How To** pray, and keep learning how to increase your faith (Luke 17:5, 6). You have a good teacher, the Holy Spirit. No matter what you have heard in the past to the contrary, let me assure you that you can learn to pray effectively and you can develop in your faith. I know this is true from my own life and I have observed this happen in the lives of other believers over several years of pastoring.

If it were all up to the Lord then he would be to blame when things went wrong in our lives. We need to learn the **How To's** that are clearly revealed in the Bible. Many of our defeats are due to our own lack of knowledge of what Christ has provided for us through Calvary. As I look back over my life I can see how I could have defeated the enemy in times past if I knew then, what I know now (John 16:12, 15). We can progress in our knowledge of the truth (Colossians 1:9). As you make time to pray and read God's words your confidence in him will grow to proportions way beyond your expectations. The devil always tries to undermine our confidence in our God and in what he has clearly promised us (Hebrews 10:19, 24, 35).

My elder daughter, Angela, went through a very difficult time when she first started secondary school – she is twelve years old at the time of writing. She would come home crying day after day, and both my wife and I spent many hours counselling her. This behaviour was totally uncharacteristic of Angela. Some of the girls at school were hard and unfriendly towards her and she did not know how to cope. I prayed for her, we spoke to the teachers at the school and yet the situation did not significantly improve.

Eventually Angela herself began to pray one hour a day, often getting up early and retiring late. She prayed and brought God's power into the situation. She came home a few weeks ago excited with the way the whole situation had completely changed: two of the girls who were upsetting her the most have become her close friends, one even approached her and asked if she could be Angela's best friend. Perhaps only those in our family could fully appreciate the great victory that came about as God answered her prayer. She is now happy and settled in her school.

Many wonderful victories await you as you develop your relationship with the Lord through prayer, and begin to learn and implement what God has revealed in the Bible.

If we want to see God's kingdom come in our lives and His will being done, we need to follow the directions that Jesus gave in Matthew 6:9 where he said *'This is how you should pray:'* The Lord's prayer is so much more than a prayer to be completed in a few seconds. There are some clear headings for prayer revealed here that we will look at in detail in another chapter.

But first let us look at the most important reason why we should pray – to get to know God better and to cultivate our relationship with Him.

Chapter 2

Prayer Brings Intimacy with God

*Jesus said 'Now this is eternal life: that they may
know you, the only true God, and Jesus Christ,
whom you have sent.'*   (John 17:3)

When we are born again we begin to get to know God.
We all know many different people at various levels of
intimacy: Think of the people you know best, they are
invariably the people with whom you have spent the
most time. Many Christians know God since he is their
Father, but at the same time they do not really know
Him intimately.

You get to know people by spending time commu-
nicating with them – it is no different with God. God
knows us, but He wants us to get to **know Him**.

Jesus said:

> *'But when you pray, go into your room, and **shut the
> door** and pray to your Father **who is in secret**; and
> your Father who sees **in secret** will reward you.'*
>
> (Matthew 6:6)

Jesus said our Father sees what is done in secret. Just
re-read that verse and stop to think about what Jesus is

saying to us. He is saying if we will take the trouble to be alone and pray, we can fellowship with the Father and more than that, the Father **will reward us**.

The word 'secret' means: kept back from knowledge of others, guarded against discovery or observation, unrevealed, hidden, secluded, etc.

Let us just think about that verse again. Jesus is saying that although the Father is in a secret place we can get into that place and develop our relationship with Him. Jesus then goes on to teach us that, as a result of our effort His Father and our Father **will reward us**.

Although the rewards are manifold, for me the greatest reward is **an inner strength**, a **sense of well being**, a **new confidence** and a **greater awareness of God**; these benefits help me to find the motivation to be alone with God.

A great man of God once said 'God has created us in such a way that we need to know the purpose and benefit of something if we are going to be motivated to work for that thing'.

To get to **know God** you **must** spend time with Him alone in prayer, and in the reading of His Word and meditating upon it. There is no other way that can be substituted to develop a really deep and fulfilling relationship with our God. No other way! Fellowship with other Christians is good and we must have it. We must belong to a good local Church under God-given leadership. We need to study the Bible systematically and regularly but there is no activity, secular or Christian, that is more necessary or more rewarding than spending time daily alone with the Lord in prayer. We should not pray at all times to the exclusion of our other responsibilities, but if we want to know God well **we must pray**.

Jesus taught his disciples

> **'Always** *pray and not give up.'*   (Luke 18:1)

Paul said:

> *'pray continually'*   (1 Thessalonians 5:17)

To me that means to pray regularly and consistently, not to pray at every instant.

In Ephesians 6:18 Paul again inspired by the Holy Spirit says:

> *'Pray in the Spirit on all occasions'.*

We Get Direction in Prayer

When we slacken off in our daily times with God we begin to lose direction, for in those times we get to know Him and we speak to Him, and He gives us revelation from the Bible. It is an awful experience for a child of God to go week after week and hear nothing from his or her God. In prayer He speaks revelation strength and direction into our lives.

In 1986 God spoke to me very clearly in a dream one night. In the dream a well-known church leader was in conversation with me. He suddenly said 'you have not been listening to the Holy Spirit – you need to take seven days to listen to the Holy Spirit', then I awoke immediately. As I lay there in the dark I began to analyse the dream. I asked myself if this was really God speaking to me or if it was just a very interesting dream. Then I remembered Acts 16:9, 10 –

> *'During the night Paul had a vision of a man of Macedonia standing and begging him, "Come over to Macedonia and help us." After Paul had seen the*

29

vision, we got ready at once to leave for Macedonia, concluding that God had called us to preach the gospel to them'.

As I pondered the content of the dream, I concluded as Paul had that God was speaking. As I also understood the call to be to a seven day fast, I assumed that it would not benefit the devil if I sought God in fasting and prayer for seven days. Shortly afterwards, I spent a week alone with the Lord in prayer and study of the Word. The Lord spoke to me very clearly on the sixth night of the fast. In the early hours of the morning He showed me some of the things that would be happening in my life in the future.

It is a wonderful thing to hear from God! It gives us such a sense of security and direction. Every Christian can and will hear from God, as he simply learns to order his life and rearrange his schedule to make prayer the number one priority.

Prayer is more important than anyone or anything in our lives. If we do not have time to pray we need to stop, re-organise and re-orientate our lives. No time to pray, in essence, means no time for God. In prayer we get to know God for ourselves. We minister to Him and He ministers to us. You will **find strength, gain confidence, receive direction and revelation**, and much more as you make prayer the number one priority in your life.

Above all, through prayer you will get to know your God and come into a new place of confidence and security in your relationship with Him. Prayer brings intimacy with God – but there is more – much more. If you have read this far, I assume that like me, you have a desire to deepen, broaden and lengthen your prayer life. Let us continue together.

Chapter 3

Prayer Changes Us

At the time of writing, Dennise and I have been married for almost fifteen years. We have certainly had our share of ups and downs in our marriage over the years. However, after almost fifteen years I love my wife in a much deeper and stronger way than ever before. In the early years of our marriage, it seemed we had a lot more downs than ups; we have been through times of severe financial hardship where we did not have sufficient money to live on for prolonged periods. I have nearly left the ministry on several occasions, and there was a time when our marriage seemed to be over. It was during these times of compounded and intense pressure, that the Lord was able to catch my attention for long enough to teach me to pray. It has not been easy but it has definitely been worth it.

I remember once many years ago, in sheer frustration, staying up at night to pray. I had tried everything I knew at the time, to bring Dennise and myself into some kind of a reasonably happy marriage, but with no success. I then did something that I had never done befor – I sat in the front room, and prayed in tongues for a whole hour and then a second, and was well on my way to three hours – it just seemed like the right thing to do. After all, it seemed I had tried everything else to no avail. As I prayed in tongues, I kept saying 'Lord you have got to change Dennise,' I said it over and over again. All of a sudden, a clear sentence of words came into my mind; it startled me as I was not really expecting an answer right away. I knew it was God speaking, He said, 'I will change her, but first I want to change you.' This was not what I wanted to hear, but it was God's word to me.

Those few words that night began to change my perspective of God, Dennise and our marriage. Those few words pointed me afresh to my responsibilities as a husband, as revealed in the Bible. They filled me with hope and faith, as I began to see what God had in mind for us as a couple. It was worth losing those hours of sleep to hear from the Lord. Many Christians do not hear from God because they are too busy to pray!

When I go before the Lord in prayer, He frequently speaks to me through Scripture. I never assume that many of the thoughts in my mind are God speaking to me – we need to be responsible in this area. Thoughts can come from many sources including our own mind and imagination, and Satan can be behind some of the thoughts which occur to us. As we develop our fellowship times with the Lord in prayer and Bible meditation we will learn to recognise when God is speaking to us. In my experience, the Lord does not always speak in a dramatic way, although He definitely does on occasions. More often than not, after a time of prayer for a person or situation, I just sense that the situation is in God's hands and that He will work it out.

As I said earlier, we need to be responsible in the area

of hearing God. It is not wrong to check and double check a revelation, and get counsel from a responsible and mature leader.

Most of the occasions that I have heard from the Lord, have been during times of prayer, or during or after a time of prayer and fasting – that in itself is a wonderful incentive for me to pray. I do not always find prayer easy – some things however are worth the effort.

When we pray, we fellowship with the Lord. We speak to Him and give Him opportunity to speak to us; into our hearts, and through the Bible. I always keep my Bible near me when I am praying. In prayer we get to know Him, and understand His ways, we get his perspective on issues, and it changes us. That is why, although it is really God who changes us, we say prayer changes us. Through prayer, we commune and fellowship with our Lord, and God is able to affect us and influence us to be changed into His likeness. A great man of God was asked 'What is the secret of your success?' His response was simple but significant: 'I pray and I obey.'

Chapter 4

How to Develop a Powerful and Effective Daily Prayer Time

In the last days, God says, I will pour out my Spirit on all people. Your sons and daughters will prophesy, your young men will see visions, your old men will dream dreams. Even on my servants, both men and women, I will pour out my Spirit in those days, and they will prophesy. (Acts 2:17, 18)

God has spoken to me in a dream on several occasions but let me state again, that I do not believe every second dream we have is from God. On average the Lord has probably spoken to me less than once a year via a dream. There are of course several instances recorded in the Bible where God has spoken to people in a dream.

In December 1987, I saw myself in a dream leading worship in a large hall. It was an evangelistic meeting featuring a well-known evangelist. The meeting was coming to an end, and while we were singing the last song I called to the evangelist telling him that I felt we should exhort the people to serious prayer. He looked at me and said 'you do it', and walked away. I got ready to quote Colossians 4:2 at the end of the song but noticed to my dismay that most people were beginning to leave the hall during the final song. By the end of the song, almost three quarters of the people had left the hall. I was rather disappointed that most folk would not hear what I was about to say as I felt it was important. However, I began to quote Colossians 4:2 and to my horror realised that I had forgotten exactly what it said. The dream ended abruptly and I awoke saying to myself, *'Continue steadfastly in prayer, being watchful in it with thanksgiving'* (Colossians 4:2).

As I awoke I recognised God was speaking to me, and one of the things He was clearly saying was that I should *'**continue** steadfastly in prayer'*, whilst especially noting the rest of the verse. I shared the dream with the members of New Life Christian Centre and we knew that God was telling us to continue in prayer and spiritual warfare and not let up.

I know that it is not always easy to pray: I have been a pastor long enough and have counselled and spoken to enough Christians in England and abroad to know that it is not always easy to pray. Many Christians can watch television for several hours a week, or socialise for long periods, or engage in numerous activities and yet not find time to pray. The devil does not mind you watching television; but he hates to see you pray. When you get to know God better you are going to be a bigger problem to him.

Some things are not easy but they are essential. A parent may not always relish shopping or cooking but it is important to do it. Prayer is essential and we need to make a time to pray each day. Out of a regular time spent with God each day will come many other good things. I will elaborate on this in a later chapter.

Dr Yonggi Cho in his excellent book 'Prayer, a Key to Revival' says: 'to guarantee our continual personal growth as a Christian, we must have a regular devotional life. If we stop praying we begin to slow down as we move from impetus to momentum.'

Naturally the first important step towards developing a daily prayer time is *to be utterly convinced of our need and the necessity for it.* We need to see that God has chosen to work on this earth through the prayers of his people. God invented prayer for our benefit!

Through prayer we fellowship with the Lord and also ask and receive from him (John 16:24; John 15:16; Luke 11:10, 11). Because God has chosen to work through His Church and through the prayers of his Church, prayer is one of the main avenues by which we exert our God-given authority over the devil. When we continue in prayerlessness we give the devil an unnecessary advantage over us. Our own prayerlessness will only encourage us to fall prey to unbelief, fear and doubt. However, through regular prayer and fellowship in the Word of God we can develop, with the right teaching, a healthy spiritual life (Jude 20).

A healthy person is not one who is down with coughs, colds, flu, fever etc., on a regular basis. Similarly a person who is spiritually healthy, who prays and absorbs the Word under a good clear Bible teaching ministry, will not be continually subject to anxiety, fear, doubt and unbelief. Can you picture any of the great heroes of our faith, such as Paul, Peter, David, Daniel, Moses or Joshua living continually in bondage to unbelief or fear? No, although they all failed at times, these men learnt how to keep themselves spiritually healthy, and lived victorious lives for the Lord. God has called us in spite of our own failures and short comings to live victorious Christian lives (1 Corinthians 15:57). To live a victorious Christian life we must develop the faith that God has gifted us with. Yes, faith comes to us as a gift when we are born again (Romans 12:3) – then it needs to be developed and used correctly (1 John 5:4, 5). However, without a regular prayer life, the growth of our faith is seriously hindered and we easily fall prey to unnecessary temptation (Romans 14:23; Matthew 26:41).

> *'Then he returned to his disciples and found them sleeping. '"Could you men not keep watch with me for one hour?" He asked Peter. "Watch and pray so that you will not fall into temptation. The spirit is willing, but the body is weak."'*
>
> (Matthew 26:40, 41)

If we have seen our need to pray, we then need to take steps to develop this discipline daily.

> *I love them that love me,*
> *and those that seek me early shall find me.*
>
> (Proverbs 8:17 AV)

Jesus mentioned the word **daily** in the Lord's prayer. I believe it is best to go to bed a bit earlier and awake well before you need to begin the activities of your day. Seek the Lord and his strength before you face the pressures and the temptations of the day. If you begin to do this daily, you and all around you will see your spiritual growth, even after just a few days.

If you do not have a successful and fulfilling way of praying I strongly recommend that you use the Lord's prayer as a pattern to follow. We will look at this pattern shortly.

I have outlined four simple steps by which we can move into effective and powerful daily times of prayer:

Step No.1: To see our need for prayer and to realise the benefits of a regular prayer life.

Step No.2: To pray and ask the lord for the desire to pray (Proverbs 10:24; Psalm 145:16, 19) – With the desire will come the motivation.

Step No.3: To set aside a time daily and develop the discipline of prayer.

Step No.4: To develop a pattern in prayer that is suited to you, so that you engage in a rounded, balanced prayer life.

Step No.1:

To see your need for prayer and to realise the benefits of a regular prayer life.

Let me now outline some of the clear benefits of regular prayer life.

a) In prayer we commune with the Lord and get to know him better. Prayer is talking with God, fellowshipping with Him, and in and through prayer we meet with the Lord and often hear from Him.

b) Through our prayer times with God we can see His divine order begin to filter into our lives. We can pray 'Thy kingdom come, thy will be done' in our lives. In prayer we can discover God's will for our lives (Matthew 6:10) and gain direction for our lives and ministries.

c) In prayer we can put our requests before the Lord and receive answers to our prayers (John 15:7; Matthew 6:11; Luke 11:9, 10; John 16:24).

d) Through prayer we can receive forgiveness and keep our hearts right with God (Matthew 6:12).

e) In prayer we can receive strength from the Lord for the Christian life. We also, are strengthened against temptation (Luke 22:40, 46).

f) Our unselfish intercession for others can radically affect their lives (Luke 22:31, 32).

g) Through prayer we can pray against evil and engage in spiritual warfare and get victory over the devil (Matthew 6:13; 2 Corinthians 10:4, 5). We can stop and break many of the ploys, plans and strategies of the evil one through aggressive warring prayer (2 Corinthians 1:10, 11; Mark 9:28, 29; Matthew 17:20, 21).

> *Praise be to the Lord, my Rock,*
> *who trains my hands for war,*
> *my fingers for battle.*   (Psalm 144:1)

Even though the above list is not exhaustive, we see neglect of prayer can result in much unnecessary suffering – prayerlessness produces lethargic, defeated Christians. Prayer is the Christian's supreme weapon. A praying warring church that is functioning correctly will always bring destruction to the armies of hell (Matthew 16:18, 19; Matthew 12:28, 29).

Step No.2:

Pray asking the Lord for the desire to pray

> *What the righteous **desire** will be granted.*
> (Proverbs 10:24b)

> *He fulfils the **desires** of those who fear him; he also hears their cry and saves them.* (Psalm 145:19)

Surely it is God's will for us to pray (Luke 18:1). Let us confidently ask the Lord to put in, or stir up in us, the desire to pray. Please allow the Holy Spirit subsequently to rearrange your schedule after praying this prayer. It may mean less television, socialising, reading etc. In the long run you will never regret any sacrifice you need to make in order for prayer to become the number one priority of your life. You may in fact find that you have ample time to engage in all the other priorities you have.

Step No.3:

Set aside a daily time and develop the discipline of prayer.

When I look back on my Christian life, I realise that God has always been speaking to me about my prayer life. As a baby Christian I set out to spend one hour with the Lord each day.

> '"Could you men not keep watch with me for one hour?" he asked Peter. "Watch and pray so that you will not fall into temptation. The **spirit** is willing, but the **body** is weak."' (Matthew 26:40, 41 NIV)

41

Billy Graham in one of his books tells the story of an Eskimo man who had two large fighting dogs – a large black one and a large white one. He had trained these dogs to fight each other. He would bring them into town, and folk would place their money on one or the other. After a while someone noticed that the Eskimo always knew beforehand which one would win: when he was asked how he knew which dog would win, his reply was very simple, he said, 'I feed one and I starve the other'.

Your spirit is willing to pray, Jesus said, it is our flesh that is weak. Little or no time in the Word and prayer, results in the flesh growing stronger – but time spent in prayer and God's Word strengthens us in our Spirit and mind to live for the Lord and serve Him effectively. Only those who have never developed a strong prayer life would try to disagree with this fact.

When I first set out to spend an hour with God I had some good advice from an excellent Christian book. At first I aimed for 15 minutes. It gradually grew to 20, then 30 and although I did fall asleep a few times along the way I found that after a few weeks I was spending one hour with the Lord each day.

I noticed a marked difference in my life almost immediately. I found I had more patience and self control and my wife must have found me easier to live with.

Find a time that suits you preferably before you face the pressures and temptations of the day and build up your time gradually. You can spend one hour with God. If you aim for an hour and settle for half an hour you will still be doing well.

I have often had people come up to me after I have taught on prayer and testify that they were able to spend quality time with the Lord when they used the pattern I recommended which is outlined in Step 4.

> *I can do everything through Him who gives me strength.* (Philippians 4:13)

Step No.4:

Develop a pattern in prayer that is suited to you so that you can engage in a rounded, balanced prayer life.

In Matthew 6:9, Jesus said *'This is how you should pray'*. Jesus outlined the way to do it.

In what we call the Lord's prayer, we have more than simply a prayer to be prayed in a minute. In it we have a pattern or a format which Jesus himself taught. *'This is how you should pray'* – Jesus said.

We see six clear sections in the Lord's prayer which are outlined below; to spend ten minutes on each section would amount to one hour. Five minutes on each would amount to half an hour.

1.   Our Father in Heaven, hallowed be your name.
Jesus taught that we should commence our times of prayer by focusing on our Heavenly Father – not on our requests. It is good to begin our prayer time with worship. Worship, praise and thank Him for all His goodness to you. To start with worship and praise is very good as it gets our focus off ourselves and on to God.

2.   Your kingdom come, Your will be done on earth as it is in Heaven.
Again it is healthy to pray for God's kingdom to come in our lives and for God's will to be done before we actually put any requests before the Lord. The kingdom of God comes wherever Jesus is King. Praying this way helps us to align our lives with God's will for us.

We can pray 'Your kingdom come in **my life, in my**

43

home and family, in my church and **leaders** and **in our nation**.'

During the ten minutes you spend on each section, you can pray and sing with your mind and your spirit as 1 Corinthians 14:15 says – *'I will pray with the spirit and I will pray with the mind also; I will sing with the spirit and I will sing with the mind also.'* Although this refers to corporate prayer and worship the principle still applies in personal prayer. So, we can pray in tongues and with our minds as well, and you have already spent twenty minutes in prayer – well done!

3. Give us today our daily bread.

At this point we can put all our requests before our loving Father who delights to hear and answer our prayers. We can ask Him for all we need in spirit and soul and body. (1 Thessalonians 5:23).

Always remember to base your requests on the promises of God. Find the scripture where God has promised you what you need and pray in line with His Word.

If you abide in me (to me that means if you are born again and are a branch in the Vine and walking before the Lord cleansed with the Blood of Jesus) ... *and my words abide in you* – We need to line up our prayers with God's Word – then ask whatever you will and it will be done for you.

I have lost count of the numerous occasions where I have prayed specifically for an issue and God has clearly and definitely answered the prayer. I was invited to speak in the United States but the air fare was not forthcoming. I consequently resorted to prayer, asking the Lord to show His approval by providing the money. I told the fellowship on Sunday that I was going that week. I suppose most people assumed that I had the money to go – but on Monday evening an envelope was put through my door with several hundred pounds in it. I went out the next day and booked my flight. Praise God – He answers prayers!

4.   Forgive us our debts/sins as we also have forgiven our debtors.

Forgiveness is a vital ingredient in our prayer life. In this period we search our hearts before God and ask his forgiveness for every sin. We must forgive others when we pray or our prayer life will be severely hindered.

> *'Jesus says, "For if you forgive men their trespasses, your heavenly Father also will forgive you; but if you do not forgive men their trespasses, neither will your Father forgive your trespasses."'*
>
> (Matthew 6:14, 15)

This section ensures that we are keeping our hearts right with God and with man. It is vital that we forgive or it leads us into all forms of spiritual bondage.

At present I have been pastoring a church for nearly 12 years and I have seen lives utterly destroyed through unforgiveness. Unforgiveness destroys you and not the person that you are angry with! If you have a problem with unforgiveness seek mature counsel as soon as you can and be prepared to forgive.

5.   Lead us not into temptation, but deliver us from evil.
It is good to pray for strength before we are tempted. This section is a good time to put on your armour as listed in Ephesians 6:10–18 (RSV).

> v:10 – *Finally, be strong in the Lord and in the strength of his might.* v:11 – *Put on the whole armour*

of God, that you may be able to stand against the wiles of the devil. v:12 – For we are not contending against flesh and blood, but against the principalities, against the powers, against the world rulers of this present darkness, against the spiritual hosts of wickedness in the heavenly places. v:13 – Therefore take the whole armour of God, that you may be able to withstand in the evil day, and having done all, to stand. v:14 – Stand therefore, having girded your loins with truth, and having put on the breastplate of righteousness, v:15 – and having shod your feet with the equipment of the gospel of peace; v:16 – above all taking the shield of faith, with which you can quench all the flaming darts of the evil one. v:17 – And take the helmet of salvation, and the sword of the Spirit, which is the word of God. v:18 – Pray at all times in the Spirit, with all prayer and supplication. To that end keep alert with all perseverance, making supplication for all the saints.

This is a time for spiritual warfare to bind and to loose (Matthew 18:18) and to pray against the strategies of the enemy you have perceived against yourself or your family, church etc. Paul expresses this mode of prayer perfectly in verse 18 of Ephesians 6.

It is not difficult to identify the areas where the enemy is trying to work against you. Any area where you are not enjoying the **'life of God'** as Jesus has promised in his Word is an area where the life flow is being blocked. If our hearts are right with God we can confidently destroy the work of the enemy as we believe God in prayer.

Jesus said we were to pray to be delivered from evil. If you have spent ten minutes on each section you have now been in prayer for 50 minutes.

6. For yours is the kingdom and the power and the glory forever, Amen.

It is good to end our prayer time as we started – with praise, and worship, focusing afresh on the greatness and the power and the glory of God and his eternal purposes for us.

We can rise from our prayer times with a fresh strength, faith and vitality to face the challenges before us, that come from Satan, self or others. We have been with God and we are ready for the day. I have noticed personally as others have said, that something supernatural happens in us when we spend an hour with God.

In summing up this chapter on developing a powerful and effective pray time I recommend that you use the Lord's prayer format at some point in your devotional time. It is the pattern Jesus taught.

My daughter Angela used to pray in English for 20 minutes, then pray about her day in tongues for 20 minutes, and then read her Bible for 20 minutes.

If you use a different devotional method that is fine, but however you approach this discipline, developing a vibrant and satisfying prayer life is crucially important – you will never regret it.

During a time of prayer with some Bible students the Lord gave me this prophecy. Even as the Lord gave it to me I trust it will be used by Him to encourage and stir you into prayer:

> 'The time is now:
> You have come to me in prayer. I've seen you in the night hours as you've come to me in prayer. And the Lord your God would reassure you, that now is the time for the fulfilment of the promises. Many of

the things I've said in days gone by, says the Lord, I will now fulfil, for you are living in the days in which I have promised to pour out my Spirit.

And I say to you my people; come to me afresh, come to me afresh and allow the spirit of prayer to come upon you. And allow me to stir you up in prayer. Come to me in the early hours of the morning. Come to me in the late hours of the night and stand before me and worship me and pray.

For I would speak into your heart things you have not known; great and wonderful things you have not known, and I will give you a vision, and I will put in your mind and in your heart my thoughts, says the Lord, the thoughts that I desire you to have – the direction in which I desire you to go.

But come to me, come aside. Spend time with me that I may minister to you even as you minister to me. And know this: **now** is the time of promise – **now** is the time of fulfilment – **now** is the day in which I will pour out my Spirit even upon you, and even upon your family and even upon this land, says the Lord.

So come aside, and allow me to stir you, and allow me to put the Spirit of prayer upon you, that those things which I purpose and desire, may come upon you and your family and this land and may be fulfilled.'

Chapter 5

Overcoming Satan with Prayer – Spiritual Warfare

In Matthew 16:18, 19 Jesus said:

> *'I will build my Church, and the gates of Hades will not overcome it. I will give you the keys of the kingdom of heaven; whatever you bind on earth will be bound in heaven, and whatever you loose on earth will be loosed in heaven.'*

In the same breath that Jesus prophesied the building of his Church, he also pointed out that there would be opposition from hell. Jesus informs us, in His enlightening dialogue with Peter, that we could subdue this opposition by using the keys He gives us and by exerting the authority over the devil given to us by our Lord.

Because Satan is a liar, a deceiver, a murderer and worse, he and his cohorts have worked overtime to deceive God's people, and to rob us of the clear realisation of our authority over him. When you meet people and have read accounts of those who have been delivered from satanism and witchcraft, you realise that Satan is no ordinary wicked being.

Some of the things Satan inspires his followers to do are so vile and disgusting that I would hesitate to print the details here. Child sacrifice, ritualistic murders, rapes and bestiality are only some of the horrific acts that we have heard of. After reading books by Christians who were delivered from Satan's clutches, and meeting some of his former followers, I began to realise that Satan is more evil than we can possibly imagine.

Having said this we are never to fear him. Many Christians are afraid of the devil! God delivered me of the fear of the devil and he will deliver you too. No, we must never fear the devil and his cohorts as they have been soundly defeated by the life, death and resurrection of Jesus Christ, and as born again believers we have authority over the works of the devil. You can break the power of evil over your life, family and home when you learn to pray effectively. Praise the Lord!

Here are some scriptures that clearly show the authority Christ has delegated to us, His Church. If you have any lingering fear of the devil memorise these scriptures and use the power in God's word to destroy your fears (Hebrews 4:12). Jesus said, *'It is the spirit that gives life, the flesh is of no avail; the words that I have spoken to you are spirit and life'* (John 6:63). I encourage you to memorise these scriptures and quote them aloud every time you feel fearful.

> **'I will give you the keys of the kingdom of heaven; and whatever you bind on earth shall be bound in heaven, and whatever you loose on earth shall be loosed in heaven.**
> (Matthew 16:10)

'All authority in heaven and on earth has been given to me. Therefore go and make disciples of all nations, baptising them in the name of the Father and of the Son and of the Holy Spirit . . . ' (Matthew 28:18–20)

'But thanks be to God! He gives us the victory through our Lord Jesus Christ.' (1 Corinthians 15:57)

'For the weapons of our warfare are not worldly but have divine power to destroy strongholds. We destroy arguments and every proud obstacle to the knowledge of God, and take every thought captive to obey Christ . . . ' (2 Corinthians 10:4, 5)

'But the Lord is faithful; He will strengthen you and guard you from evil.' (2 Thessalonians 3:3)

'For whatever is born of God overcomes the world; and this is the victory that overcomes the world, our faith.' (1 John 5:4)

'And they have conquered Him by the blood of the lamb and by the word of their testimony.'

(Revelation 12:11)

'Fear not, for I am with you, be not dismayed, for I am your God; I will strengthen you, I will help you, I will uphold you with my victorious right hand. Behold, all who are incensed against you shall be put to shame and confounded; those who strive against you shall be as nothing and shall perish. You shall seek those who contend with you but you shall not find them; those who war against you shall be as nothing at all for I, the Lord your God hold your right hand; it is I who say to you, "Fear not, I will help you"'.

(Isaiah 41:10, 13)

'No weapon that is fashioned against you shall pros-
per, and you shall confute every tongue that rises
against you in judgment. This is the heritage of the
servants of the Lord and their vindication from me,
says the Lord'.   (Isaiah 54:17)

We are living in an evil age (Galatians 1:4). Satan with
the support of fallen angels and demons is out to steal
and destroy wherever he is able. By depending on God's
power, released through prayer, we are able to break
Satan's power.

In the early days of my ministry, I did not know how
to engage in serious spiritual warfare, but after learning
how to pray and fast and bind the devil, I have seen
many situations changed by the power of fervent prayer.
We have seen many victories and lives changed as
groups of people have engaged in spiritual warfare on
behalf of another. We must be skilled in using the
weapons that God has placed at our disposal.

Terry Law in his outstanding book, 'The Power of
Praise and Worship' teaches that we have three main
weapons against the enemy. He says, 'There are three
primary weapons God has given to every believer. They
have an intrinsic power in them that is generated by the
Holy Spirit. The three weapons are: **The Word of God**;
The Name of Jesus; and **The Blood of Jesus**'. The teaching in this book is excellent and I strongly recommend it.

Terry Law goes on to explain that strongholds
(2 Corinthians 10:4) can be broken as we launch our
weapons, like nuclear warheads, using spiritual launching rockets. He explains that it is the nuclear warheads
on a rocket that do the damage and not the rockets
themselves; he likens the Name of Jesus, the Word of

God and the Blood of Jesus to the nuclear warheads. He says the spiritual launching rockets by which we launch the weapons are: **1. Prayer 2. Preaching 3. Testimony 4. Praise and Worship.** He elaborates on the teaching very clearly in his book, but as prayer is our main focus in this study I will concentrate on this aspect at present.

Just a few days ago, Pauline, a member of New Life Christian Centre came up for prayer. She had a flow of blood from her womb following a recent operation. She stated that she had been bleeding continually despite all her efforts to stop it. At the end of our service, with the presence and anointing of God upon me, I simply commanded the bleeding to cease in the Name of Jesus. Pauline phoned the next day to testify that the flow of blood had completely ceased. I am sure that thousands, if not millions, of Christians can testify to answers to prayers as they have used **The Name**, **The Word** and **The Blood** to good effect in spiritual warfare.

When the **'Name of Jesus'** is used in simple faith the works of the devil can be destroyed (John 14:12, 14; Acts 10:38). Jesus quoted the written **'Word'** at the devil and put him to flight (Matthew 4:1, 11). In Revelation 12:11 we read how Satan was overcome by *'the blood of the lamb'* and by the words of testimony. I believe as we speak or testify about what the blood of Jesus has done for us and as we use this testimony in prayer it is a tremendous weapon against Satan.

We need to discover our weapons and learn to use them, in faith, against the plans, ploys and strategies of the enemy. As we persist in prayer using our authority in the Name of Jesus, using the power that is in God's Word and testifying to the merits of the blood of Jesus, many great victories await us.

Prayer in the Context of Spiritual Warfare

'Finally be strong in the Lord and in the strength of His might. Put on the whole armour of God, that you may be able to stand against the wiles of the devil. For we are not contending against flesh and blood, but against the principalities, against the powers, against the world rulers of this present darkness, against the spiritual hosts of wickedness in heavenly places. Therefore take the whole armour of God, that you may be able to withstand in the evil day, and having done all, to stand. Stand therefore, having girded your loins with truth, and having put on the breastplate of righteousness, and having shod your feet with the equipment of the gospel of peace; above all taking the shield of faith, with which you can quench all the flaming darts of the evil one. And take the helmet of salvation, and the sword of the spirit, which is the word of God. Pray at all times in the spirit with all prayer and supplication. To that end keep alert with all perseverance, making supplication for all the saints.' (Ephesians 6:10, 18)

The above scripture shows vividly the believer's strength, armour and enemy. The armour that Paul describes in this passage is largely defensive, with the exception of the sword of the Spirit which is the word of God. One thing I had never noticed before, even after reading this passage for several years, was that verse 18 is a key verse in the passage.

Pray at all times in the spirit with all prayer and supplication. To that end keep alert with all perseverance, making supplication for all the saints.

It is prayer – serious, fervent, alert, persevering prayer that really does the damage in pushing back the powers of darkness. In that sense, you could say that one of the primary purposes for the armour is that it is to be used in prayer. In summary Ephesians 6:10, 18 tells us to put on the whole armour of God and pray with all kinds of prayer. We are told to keep alert with all perseverance and to pray especially for other Christians.

In our churches we need to consistently pray for the other people in our fellowship. We need to not only pray inwards for our brothers and sisters in Christ but also pray outwards for the success of the Gospel message to change and transform the lives of those around us.

I believe every church needs to do both; some churches are always praying outward and the devil causes serious internal problems. Other churches are only praying inward and become insular, insignificant and ineffectual in reaching the community. We need to pray for the saints (in the church) and for the sinners outside the church. Then as the healthy, prayed over, believers go out to reach the lost, God will give the increase. Hallelujah!

A Clear Picture of Spiritual Warfare

I don't know about you but in spite of the detail referred to in Ephesians 6, I still wanted more insight into spiritual warfare. The Lord used the following passage to give a little more illumination. The illumination came through another minister whom I heard teaching on the subject.

23 – In the course of those many days the King of Egypt died. And the people of Israel groaned under their bondage, and cried out for help, and their cry under bondage came up to God. 24 – and God heard their groaning, and God remembered His covenant with Abraham, with Isaac and with Jacob. 25 – and God saw the people of Israel, and God knew their condition. (Exodus 3:23–25)

1 – Now Moses was keeping the flock of his father-in-law, Jethro, the priest of Midian; and he led his flock to the west side of the wilderness and came to Horeb, the mountain of God. 2 – And the Angel of the Lord appeared to him in a flame of fire out of the midst of a bush; and he looked, and lo! the bush was burning, and yet it was not consumed. 3 – And Moses said, 'I will turn aside and see this great sight why the bush is not burnt'. 4 – When the Lord saw that he turned aside to see, God called to him out of the bush, 'Moses, Moses!' and he said, 'Here Am I'. 5 – Then he said, 'Do not come near; put off your shoes from your feet, for the place on which you are standing is holy ground'. 6 – And he said, 'I am the God of your Father, the God of Abraham, the God of Isaac, and the God of Jacob.' And Moses hid his face, for he was afraid to look at God. 7 – Then the Lord said, 'I have seen the affliction of my people who are in Egypt, and have heard their cry because of their taskmasters; I know their sufferings, 8 – and I have come down to deliver them out of the hand of the Egyptians, and to bring them up out of that land to a good and broad land, a land flowing with milk and honey, to the place of the Canaanites, the Hittites, the Amorites, the Perizzites, the Hivites, and the Jebusites'. (Exodus 3:1–8)

In this passage, God informs Moses that He has seen the suffering of the Israelites and that he intends to deliver them from the Egyptians and bring them into a good, broad land flowing with milk and honey (verse 8). The land is clearly very good, but it is also a place where the Canaanites, Hittites, Amorites, Perizzites, Hivites and Jebusites dwell.

Joshua took over from Moses and led the Israelites into the fulfilment of the promises (Joshua 1:1, 9).

> *After the death of Moses the servant of the Lord, the Lord said to Joshua the son of Nun, Moses' minister, 'Moses my servant is dead; now therefore arise, go over this Jordan, you and all this people, into the land which I am giving to them, to the people of Israel. Every place that the sole of your foot will tread upon I have given to you. As I promised to Moses.'*
> (Joshua 1:1, 3)

The land had been promised to them – prophetically it was theirs – but they had to go in with faith and courage putting aside fear and doubt and unbelief and take what was rightfully theirs.

Can you picture the Canannites, Amorites and all the other 'ites' saying to Joshua – 'Well OK, Joshua old chap, now let us be reasonable about this. You say God has promised you this land? – Well alright! Now just give us a day or two to pack all our belongings – There's the milk; there's the honey; help yourself old fellow, and by the way, there are some grapes here as well. Just give us a couple of days and we'll be off and then it's all yours – all the milk, land, honey, grapes etc. etc.'

Needless to say the 'ites' made them fight for the land.

When they moved forward courageously and with faith, God gave them the victory. Many great victories were won by Joshua and his troops.

In the New Testament it says we **wrestle not** against flesh and blood. In the Old Testament they did fight against flesh and blood – but now in the New Testament we are wrestling against **principalities, powers, world rulers and spiritual wickedness** in high places.

The Old Testament gives us the picture of real war. David and Joshua and others fought – God gave them the victory.

There were times, as with **Jehoshaphat** (2 Chronicles 20) and with **Jericho** (Joshua 6) that God gave his people a special strategy for victory. But most of the time they had to go in there and fight and win and afterwards they would say that 'God gave them the victory'.

When the Philistines heard that David had been anointed King over Israel, all the Philistines went up in search of David; but David heard of it and went down to the stronghold. Now the Philistines had come and spread out in the valley of Rephaim. And David inquired of the Lord, 'Shall I go up against the Philistines? Wilt thou give them into my hand?'. And the Lord said to David, 'Go up; for I will certainly give the Philistines into your hand' and David came to Baal-Perazim, and David defeated them there; and he said, 'The Lord has broken through my enemies before me, like a bursting flood'. (2 Samuel 5:17, 25)

We are More Than Conquerors

After the victory that Jesus won through the cross, we

are operating as **more than conquerors** (Romans 8:37) because Christ has defeated the devil:

> *'When I saw him, I fell at his feet as though dead. But he laid his right hand upon me, saying, "Fear not, I am the first and the last, and the living one; I died, and behold I am alive for evermore, and **I have the keys of death and Hades**".'* (Revelation 1:17, 18)

This means that we are enforcing a victory that has already taken place. That is why we are **more than** conquerors! But even though the victory has taken place, it has to be enforced.

We enforce this victory over that cheat and liar, the devil, with violence. Spiritual warfare is aggressive. Do not allow the devil to trespass in your life or family. Drive him out by taking authority over him in the Name of Jesus and by dedicating yourself to aggressive prayer.

Just as you learn to play tennis or golf by actually playing the game you will learn to pray aggressively and effectively, by getting down to prayer. You can read all the theory of tennis and read every book available on the game but you will never learn to play until you get on to a court and hit the ball. I used to be a club tennis player myself. Coaching will help, but you have to get on the court and play. Once you begin to get competent at returning the ball, you can begin to learn and develop your tactical play.

Spiritual warfare involves the tactical side of prayer. Many Christians never go beyond the first stage which is to actually set aside regular times to pray. God wants to teach us to defeat the devil so that we can rejoice and shout in victory just as Joshua, David and others fought, won and greatly rejoiced over their victories.

We are in a war whether we like it or not. By developing our faith, rising up in prayer and using our spiritual weapons we will be able to put the enemy to flight over and over again.

Start out right where you are and, with faith in God, take authority over the devil and drive him from your life, home and family. We need to be sensible and grow in maturity in this area. You and I cannot bind up every devil over London or England, or whichever country you happen to be in. That is a job for the whole Church of Jesus in the nation. Start off where you are and grow in your faith. Churches praying corporately can exert great power over a given area and beyond. There is much to learn in this area, but let's start out realistically and grow in strength in this area.

Desperate situations require desperate measures! When a marriage is on the brink of divorce, make no mistake the devil had his hand in it somewhere. When a son or daughter is flirting with the world or a church is about to split – these are desperate situations. They will not change with a five minute prayer meeting followed by biscuits and tea. This is not a time for a few minutes prayer in between your favourite television programmes. Desperate situations require earnest prayer.

These are times to rise early and spend extended periods in prayer warring violently against the devil. These are times to pray into the early hours of the morning crying out to God to release his power to defeat satanic forces. These are times to join together with others and pray that God will overturn the enemy's plans. Yes, some situations even require fasting and prayer to demolish evil strongholds.

Chapter 6

Prayer and Fasting

This is the chapter that I am the most excited about writing. When fasting and prayer are engaged in correctly, it probably does more damage to the enemy than any other weapon in the Christian armoury.

You could say that fasting and prayer are the atomic bomb in the Christian's weaponry which, when understood and used effectively destroys demonic strongholds like no other weapon.

> 'Is not this the fast that I choose:
> to loose the bonds of wickedness,
> to undo the thongs of the yoke,
> and let the oppressed go free,
> and to break every yoke?'   (Isaiah 58:6)

There are of course many reasons for fasting revealed in the Bible. It is not a cure-all or a way to twist God's arm but to me the Bible is very clear on the subject. Fasting and praying do not change God, they change us and I believe that every Christian, in normal health, needs to be involved in this great Christian discipline.

Dr. Paul Yonggi Cho says: 'As we learn how to pray in

the Holy Spirit, realising that we have been given the authority, we are able to bind the forces of Satan in people, communities and even nations. However, because Satan is a liar and the father of lies, he tries to convince us that he is in control. But as we learn to fast and pray and exercise our rightful spiritual authority, Satan and his forces must yield to the will of God.'

For a long time I was reluctant to share any of my experiences in fasting and prayer because of my understanding of the biblical admonition that fasting was to remain a secret between ourselves and the Lord. Then I began to realise that we could share some of our experiences in this area in order to teach others, as long as our motives are pure. I still, however, believe that personal fasting, at the time we engage in it, should be between us and God alone.

The 40 day fast of Jesus is recorded in Scripture, so we know that Jesus mentioned it, perhaps afterwards, to his followers. Also the fasts of Daniel, David, Moses, Paul and others are recorded in Scripture – for example:

> *'Then Jesus was led up by the Spirit into the wilderness to be tempted by the Devil. And he fasted forty days and forty nights, and afterward he was hungry.'*
> (Matthew 4:1, 2)

After this fast Jesus effectively began his ministry. Luke 4:1 records that Jesus was full of the Holy Spirit – Luke 4:14 says Jesus returned in the power of the Spirit – after fasting

> *'And for three days he* [Saul] *was without sight, and neither ate nor drank.'*
> (Acts 9:9)

> '*Now in the church at Antioch there were prophets and teachers, Barnabas, Symeon who was called Niger, Lucius of Cyrene, Manaen a member of the court of Herod the Tetarch, and Saul. While they were worshipping the Lord and fasting, the Holy Spirit said, "Set apart for me Barnabas and Saul for the work to which I have called them". Then after fasting and praying they laid their hands on them and sent them off.*' (Acts 13:1–3 RSV)

I shared in an earlier chapter how the Lord called me to a seven day fast in a dream. On the sixth night of the fast God spoke to me very clearly giving me direction for my life and ministry. God has often been very gracious to speak to me clearly during times of fasting and prayer. I do not know if I could have survived the pressures of the ministry without those clear words from Him.

Several years ago we had some serious problems in our fellowship. At the time, my wife was visiting her family in Canada along with our two youngest children, John and Sarah. As Dennise was away for seven weeks, it presented me with a good opportunity to undertake a longer fast.

My good friend and fellow minister, Doug Williams was staying with me at the time, and together we embarked on a 20 day fast. During this time, with God's help, I continued in most of my pastoral duties of preaching, visiting etc. God moved and turned things around in our church situation and this fast marked a turning point in the ministry.

I believe every Christian should try to develop the simple discipline of fasting at least one day a week, and that ministers should engage in fasting regularly, to see the power and the anointing of God consistently manifest in their ministry.

There are many good books on this subject some of which are named at the back of this book. The common sense and practical guidelines for fasting should be carefully observed.

The Definition of Fasting

We could say that fasting is the practice of deliberately abstaining from food for spiritual purposes
– or – fasting is voluntary and deliberate abstinence from food for the purpose of concentrated prayer.

Fasting is a spiritual discipline much neglected by the church due to ignorance on the subject. 'To fast' means primarily not to eat – the purpose being to humble ourselves before God; to give Him our undivided attention; to be sensitive to His voice and receptive to His power; to place ourselves in a position where we are utterly at his disposal. Therefore, fasting is an abstinence from earthly food in order to feast on the heavenly. The best starting point for a study of the Christian discipline of fasting is found in the sermon on the mount.

Matthew 6:1–18 – Jesus said: **when** you give alms (verses 2, 3); **when** you pray (verses 5, 6); **when** you fast (verses 16, 17).

By using the word '**when**' rather than '**if**' Jesus assumes that we will practice the disciplines of giving, praying and fasting. There is, of course, a difference between private prayer and fasting, and the corporate and public practices. Private prayer and times of fasting should be done in secret to avoid the temptation of spiritual pride.

> *'And when you fast, do not look dismal, like the hypocrites, for they disfigure their faces that their fasting may be seen by men. Truly, I say to you, they have their reward, but when you fast, anoint your head and wash your face, that your fasting may not be seen by men but by your Father who is in secret; and your Father who sees in secret will reward you.'*
> (Matthew 6:16–18)

However, there are also many examples in Scripture of public and proclaimed fasts and these by their very nature are done openly and not in secret.

Corporate Fasting

> *Then Jehoshaphat feared, and set himself to seek the Lord, and proclaimed a fast throughout all Judah. And Judah assembled to seek help from the Lord; from all the cities of Judah they came to seek the Lord.* (2 Chronicles 20:3, 4)

> *'"Go, gather all the Jews to be found in Susa, and hold a fast on my behalf, and neither eat nor drink for three days, night or day. I and my maids will also fast as you do. Then I will go to the King, though it is against the law; and if I perish, I perish". 17 – Mordecai then went away and did everything as Esther had ordered him.'* (Esther 4:16, 17)

Tremendous results followed these above mentioned fasts.

A couple of years ago I called the members of our fellowship to a week of fasting and prayer. We drew out a seven day chart and different members chose the days that suited them. Some fasted for a day some for three days others fasted for all seven days. The proclaimed fast was voluntary but a good percentage of folk got involved. We fasted and prayed for the fellowship and for our 'Healing Service' the following Sunday. We had a tremendous service that Sunday with remarkable deliverances and healing taking place in people's lives.

As we engage in prayer and fasting, God's power is released in deliverance and the overthrow of the enemy.

The Three Main Types of Fasting

1. The normal fast (abstaining from food). (Matthew 4:2)
2. The partial fast. (Daniel 10:2)
3. The absolute fast (maximum of 72 hours) abstaining from food and drink. (Esther 4:16; Acts 9:9)

The Normal Fast

> *'And he fasted forty days and forty nights, and afterward he was hungry.'* (Matthew 4:2)

It is generally agreed by authorities on this subject that Jesus did not eat, but that he must have drunk water. It says he was hungry, not thirsty. If Jesus had not drunk any liquids his fast would not have been a natural one as it is not possible, apart from a miracle, to exist for so long without liquids. Moses engaged in two forty day fasts but these were miraculous and supernatural as he neither ate nor drank (Deuteronomy 9:9). God's presence and power sustained him.

However it is not advisable to engage in long fasts without the clear leading of the Lord.

In summary, a normal fast consists of abstaining from solids but still drinking water. If we have fruit juice or tea etc., the fast would then come under the next category, a partial fast.

If you have never fasted before I would recommend that you miss a couple of meals and spend that time in prayer. Soon you could easily engage in a 24 hour fast going from dinner time to dinner time or breakfast to breakfast, gradually extending the fast.

Dr. Cho says: 'Normally I teach my people to begin to fast three days. Once they have become accustomed to three day fasts they will be able to fast for a period of seven days; then they will move to 10 day fasts. Some have even gone for 40 days, but this is not usually encouraged. We have seen that fasting and prayer causes one to become spiritually sensitive to the Lord, causing more power in one's life to combat the forces of Satan'.

It is important to break our fasts in the correct manner following the guidelines mentioned in the many good books on the subject – (see section on practical points for fasting).

The Partial Fast

> *In those days I, Daniel, was mourning for three weeks. I ate no delicacies, no meat or wine entered my mouth, nor did I anoint myself at all for the full three weeks.* (Daniel 10:2, 3)

It would appear that Daniel engaged in a partial fast for three weeks; after this he was visited by an Angel who revealed to him the reason for the delay to the answer of his prayer.

> *'Then he said to me, "Fear not, Daniel, for from the first day that you set your mind to understand and humbled yourself before your God, your words have been heard, and I have come because of your words. The Prince of the Kingdom of Persia withstood me twenty one days; but Michael, one of the chief princes, came to help me, so I left him there with the Prince of the Kingdom of Persia and came to make you understand what is to befall your people in the latter days. For the vision is for days yet to come."'*
>
> (Daniel 10:12–14)

After three weeks of Daniel's prayer and fasting the angel was able to break through the satanic opposition in the heavenlies (Ephesians 2:3). Daniel's prayers were clearly needed to cause the effective breakthrough.

Jesus taught that some types of demonic strongholds can only be broken by prayer and fasting (Matthew 17:18–21; Mark 9:14–29).

We can engage in partial fasts in the following manner:

a) Fruit juice fasts (fruit juice at meal times)
b) Tea and coffee (at meal times – not recommended for health reasons)
c) One light meal a day (being careful to keep it light).

I felt the leading the Lord while I was in secular employment, many years ago to engage in a three week partial fast eating one light meal a day.

A partial fast therefore is when we consume anything other than water. This type of fast has its place and can be recommended at times. When I engaged in a seven day fast, mentioned earlier, I drank fruit juices at meal times.

The Absolute Fast: Esther 4:16, Acts 9:9

> *'And for three days he was without sight, and neither ate nor drank'.* (Acts 9:9)

Saul, later Paul, began his ministry with an absolute fast. In the fast he had a vision and at the end of the fast he was healed and filled with the Holy Spirit (Acts 9:9, 19).

Colin Whittaker in his inspiring book, 'Prayer Mountains' says of Paul: 'Fasting helps to put the body in its place – as the soul's servant, not its master. The Apostle Paul could probably have claimed not only to "speak with tongues more than all" (1 Corinthians 14:18) but also to "fast more than all", because he could write that throughout his apostleship he had been "in fastings often"' (2 Corinthians 11:27).

It is noteworthy that he also put fastings (in the plural), high up on his list of things which helped to make him out as a true minister of Christ (2 Corinthians 6:4, 5). How many ministers can put that on their C.V.?

Daniel, David, Moses, Nehemiah, Esther, Ezra, Joel, Paul and many others all engaged in fasting towards God's higher purposes. How about you?

Some Benefits of Fasting:

1. In fasting, we humble ourselves before God allowing him to search our hearts exposing sins and wrong motives (Psalm 35:13)
2. Through fasting and prayer, the power of the Devil over people, families, churches, cities, and even nations can be broken.

3. It is a way by which we can bring the body under subjection (1 Corinthians 9:27). Pastor Jack Hayford states that he fasts at times to simply bring the flesh under control. Our body with its physical organs and appetites make a wonderful servant but a terrible master. Dr. Derek Prince says: 'Fasting deals with two great barriers to the Holy Spirit that are erected by man's carnal nature. These are: **the stubborn self-will of the soul** and **the insistent self-gratifying appetites of the body**. Rightly practised fasting brings both soul and body under subjection to the Holy Spirit. It is important to understand that fasting changes man not God. God, of course, can work more powerfully through a changed person.

4. Fasting gives greater spiritual clarity. As we feed on God's Word in times of fasting, it is not unusual to experience clearer direction and increased revelation.

5. Fasting can bring deliverance and victory. Many have testified to have received healing and deliverance during, or at the end of a time of prayer and fasting.

Corporate prayer and fasting can even lead into times of revival and a fresh outpouring of the Holy Spirit. As more and more churches enter into times of prayer and fasting together, I believe we will see a greater outpouring of the Holy Spirit in our land.

Note the progression in the following scriptures:

> *'Sanctify a fast, call a solemn assembly. Gather the elders and all the inhabitants of the land to the house of the Lord your God; and cry to the Lord.'*
>
> (Joel 1:14)

> *'"Yet even now", says the Lord, "return to me with all your heart, with fasting, with weeping, and with mourning."'* (Joel 2:12)

> *'Blow the trumpet in Zion; sanctify a fast; call a solemn assembly; gather the people.*
> *Sanctify the congregation; assemble the elders; gather the children, even nursing infants.*
> *Let the bridegroom leave his room, and the bride her chamber.'* (Joel 2:15, 16)

> *'And it shall come to pass afterward, that I will pour out my spirit on all flesh; your sons and your daughters shall prophesy, your old men shall dream dreams, and your young men shall see visions.'*
> (Joel 2:28)

Some Guidelines and Practical Points for Fasting

1. Enter into your fast with positive faith. Give plenty of time to feed on God's Word.

2. Aim for specific objectives in fasting. Write them down – expect the answers and give thanks when the answers are received.

3. Guard against pride or boasting while fasting. Keep your motives pure and search your heart before God. It can be a great time of spiritual cleansing.

4. If you are not in normal health and are on any kind of medication it is best to seek medical advice before engaging in a fast.

5. Avoid hot baths on longer fasts as this can cause dizziness – use lukewarm water.

6. Give yourself to prayer whenever you can. If you are working – pray in your lunch hour or set aside

71

time in the morning or evening to pray. Simply fasting with your normal quiet time can in itself be beneficial as fasting helps to subdue the flesh.

7. Break your fast gradually. The longer your period of fasting, the more care is needed to break it. At this point we need self control. After a short fast, begin with a light meal – soup and bread and chew the bread well. Ease gradually into your normal eating habits. The longer the fast the longer we should take to return to our normal pattern of eating.

8. There are many balanced books on the Christian market. Before engaging in a longer fast study the techniques in these books carefully.

Recommended Reading

1. *God's Chosen Fast* – Arthur Wallis
2. *Shaping History Through Prayer and Fasting* – Derek Prince
3. *Prayer, Key to Revival* – Paul Yonggi Cho
4. *Common Sense Guide to Fasting* – Derek Prince
5. *Prayer Mountains* – Colin Whittaker

Prayer

'Lord teach me how to fast and pray. Help me to learn, and teach me how to become a prayer warrior for you. Thank you Lord. Amen.'

Chapter 7

The Power of Corporate Prayer

'All these with one accord devoted themselves to prayer, together the women and Mary the mother of Jesus, and with his brothers'. (Acts 1:14)

Ten days before the feast of Pentecost a group of one hundred and twenty people met together for prayer. The verse above says they **'devoted'** themselves to prayer. After several days of fervent prayer the Holy Spirit of God was poured out as never before, and a great revival ushered in the beginning of the church era.

There are, of course, numerous situations recorded in the Bible where God moved in power to upset the plans of the enemy, as groups of peole prayed fervently together.

Let's look again at the tremendous promise God personally delivered to Solomon in 2 Chronicles 7:11–14:

11 – *Thus Solomon finished the house of the Lord and the king's house; all that Solomon had planned to do in the house of the Lord and in his own house he successfully accomplished.* **12** – *Then the Lord* *appeared to Solomon in the night and said to him: 'I have heard your prayer, and have chosen this place for myself as a house of sacrifice. 13 – When I shut up the heavens so that there is no rain, or command the locust to devour the land, or send pestilence among my people, 14 – if my people who are called by my name humble themselves, and pray and seek my face, and turn from their wicked ways, then I will hear from heaven, and will forgive their sin and heal their land.*

In verse 14, God gave Solomon a promise for Israel that if they humbled themselves and prayed and searched their hearts in repentance before Him, this would result in Healing and forgiveness for a whole nation.

Although this promise was made to Solomon for Israel, God revealed, in principle, that he would move, even to restore an entire Nation, if his people would earnestly seek him in prayer.

The prophet Jonah did not fully understand that God would even spare the Gentile city of Nineveh, when they turned to Him in repentance and prayer (Jonah 4:6–10).

6 – Then tidings reached the King of Nineveh, and he arose from his throne, removed his robe and covered himself with sackcloth, and sat in ashes. 7 – And he made proclamation and published through Nineveh, 'By the decree of the King and his nobles: let neither man nor beast, herd nor flock, taste anything; let them not feed, or drink water, 8 – But let man and beast be covered with sackcloth, and let them cry mightily to God; yea, let every one turn from his evil way and from the violence which is in his hands. **9 –** *Who knows, God may yet repent and turn from his fierce anger, so that we perish not?* **10 –** *When God saw what they did, how they turned from their evil way, God repented of the evil which he had said he would do to them; and he did not do it.*

(Jonah 3:6–10)

In this case, a whole city was saved from destruction through corporate prayer, fasting and repentance.

As people gather together in prayer, great power is unleashed. However, we may not always be able to gather together with a large group to pray. Let us examine the words of Jesus in Matthew 18:19–20.

19 – *'Again I say to you, if two of you agree on earth about anything they ask, it will be done for them by my Father in heaven.* **20 –** *For where two or three are gathered in my name, there am I in the midst of them'.*

One of the great joys of my life, is to meet together to pray with my two associate pastors, Robert Elliott and David Lamb. Both these men are men of faith and prayer. When we unite together to pray for our Church, God always moves in power to turn circumstances around. We have prayed together for periods as short as an hour, and God has moved to completely change the situations or people we have prayed for. United prayer can be mightily used of God to fulfil his purposes. When even two or three pray together in unity, God can mightily use that prayer to fulfil.

A few years ago, God spoke to my heart to start up nights of prayer every Friday. I called the people of the

'New Life Christian Centre' to prayer. It seemed like the devil did everything in his power to stop these meetings. Through much pressure, we continued faithfully week after week. Sometimes we would pray from 8 p.m. till midnight, sometimes we prayed from 10 p.m. till 2 a.m., sometimes we prayed until the early hours of the morning.

When I look back I see that this period marked a new beginning in our church: The presence of God was much stronger in our meetings, a new sense of authority came into my ministry, our worship entered new dimensions of liberty and more people began to be healed, delivered and saved.

Satan knows the power of united prayer and he fears it greatly. He will try every trick to stop people and churches engaging in serious prayer. Often in our times of prayer at New Life Christian Centre, we will put our requests before the Lord in English and even pray certain scriptures over the Church such as Ephesians 4:1–16, turning the scripture into a prayer – then we will pray in tongues together for an hour. During this time we keep the prayer continuous, not stopping for anything. Any revelations, scriptures, thoughts etc. can be shared at the end of the hour.

When small or large groups pray together in tongues it is very powerful. **Tongues are given to us to use in prayer** but most Christians never enter into this dimension of praying. Let us examine some scriptures on the issue.

For one who speaks in a tongue speaks not to men but to God; (speaking to God is prayer) *For no one understands him, but he utters mysteries in the spirit.*
(1 Corinthians 14:2)

Tongues are one of the main ways that we enter into praying in the Spirit.

> *He who speaks in a tongue edifies himself.*
> (1 Corinthians 14:4)

We are definitely built up in our inner man when we speak in tongues. Paul goes on to say that in contrast, prophesy builds up the Church. Both have a separate function and are needed. When we are edified or built up we become more sensitive to the Spirit of God.

> *For if I pray in a tongue my spirit prays.*
> (1 Corinthians 14:14)

Praying in tongues is a whole new dimension in prayer.

Am I saying that if you do not pray in tongues, you cannot pray effectively? No – tongues does not make you better than anyone else, it just makes *you* **better**! Whatever dimension you have reached in prayer – tongues will enlarge your capacity further.

I often pray in tongues for long periods and I really thank God for this wonderful gift. Paul said he wanted everyone to have this gift (1 Corinthians 14:5) – Not everyone has the public gift of speaking in tongues (1 Corinthians 12:28–30), but all can receive this precious gift of God to be used in prayer and intercession.

I was invited to minister at a four day convention in Germany in 1989. I stayed with a family who went out to work during the day. As the meetings took place in the evenings I had a great deal of time to myself during the day. With not much else to do in a foreign country I spent prolonged periods in prayer and meditation, praying several hours in tongues, being edified and built up in faith. When I got to the meeting each night I saw God move in a mighty way saving, healing and delivering many from demonic bondage.

In Acts 2:42 we read: *And they devoted themselves to the apostles' teaching and fellowship, to the breaking of bread and prayers.*

Prayer is not done in isolation from other necessary activities. The early Church engaged in prayer, but also in teaching, fellowship and the breaking of bread. As corporate prayer is such a powerful tool in the hands of God to bring about his purposes, it is essential that we engage in it under the wing of responsible and mature leaders. A praying Church will see tremendous results as they engage in faithful, regular, well directed prayer. Prayer meetings need good leadership if they are to be successful.

The early Church was a dynamic, effective Church, that continued to grow at a tremendous rate. We see further examples of united prayer in Acts 4 and Acts 6 with corresponding results but perhaps my favourite scripture in this vein is Acts 12:1–17.

> *About that time Herod the King laid violent hands upon some who belonged to the Church.* **2** – *he killed James the brother of John with the sword;* **3** – *and when he saw that it pleased the Jews, he proceeded to arrest Peter also. This was during the days of unleavened bread.* **4** – *And when he had seized him, he put him in prison, and delivered him to four squads of soldiers to guard him, intending after the passover to bring him out to the people.* **5** – *So Peter*

was kept in prison; **(but earnest prayer for him was made to God by the church).** *6 – The very night when Herod was about to bring him out, Peter was sleeping between two soldiers, bound with two chains, and sentries before the door were guarding the prison; 7 – And behold, an angel of the Lord appeared, and a light shone in the cell; and he struck Peter on the side and woke him saying, 'Get up quickly.' And the chains fell off his hands. 8 – And the angel said to him, 'Dress yourself and put on your sandals.' And he did so. And he said to him, 'Wrap your mantle around you and follow me.' 9 – And he went out and followed him; he did not know that what was done by the angel was real, but thought he was seeing a vision. 10 – When they had passed the first and the second guard, they came to the iron gate leading into the city. It opened to them of its own accord, and they went out and passed on through one street; and immediately the angel left him. 11 – And Peter came to himself, and said, 'Now I am sure that the Lord has sent his angel and rescued me from the hand of Herod and from all that the Jewish people were expecting.' 12 – When he realised this, he went to the house of Mary, the mother of John whose other name was Mark,* **(where many were gathered together and were praying).** *13 – And when he knocked at the door of the gateway, a maid named Rhoda came to answer. 14 – Recognising Peter's voice, in her joy she did not open the gate but ran in and told that Peter was standing at the gate. 15 – They said to her, 'You are mad.' But she insisted that it was so. They said 'It is his angel!' 16 – But Peter continued knocking; and when they opened, they* *saw him and were amazed. **17** – But motioning to them with his hand to be silent, he described to them how the Lord had brought him out of the prison. And he said, 'Tell this to James and to the brethren.' Then he departed and went to another place.*

Herod had murdered James and had similar intentions for Peter: verse 5 ... but earnest prayer for him was made to God by the Church; verse 12 ... where many were gathered together and were praying.

Through their united prayers, God worked supernaturally and sent an angel to deliver Peter. In my opinion, if the church had started praying earnestly earlier it would have saved James' life. Herod murdered James – this was clearly not God's perfect will; a God who has commanded 'Thou shalt not kill', would not have agreed with Herod's evil intentions. Behind Herod, satanic forces were at work to destroy the church. They were defeated against Peter by serious, united, powerful, prayer!

I believe with all my heart, that lives can be saved as the saints of God engage in serious prayer. In these days God is calling leaders and churches to fervent warring prayer. The enemy is on the warpath but the Church, using the weaponry God has given, can frustrate his plans as we rise up together and pray.

On 27th February 1990, I was lecturing in a Bible School in a class of about 60 students. As I normally do I asked the students to start to pray for about five minutes, before the lecture. There were a lot of new students in the class, and I remembered that this class had been a bit slow to pray when I was with them the previous week.

We stood to pray and after praying in English we went

into praying in tongues together. To my surprise, ten minutes later nearly all the students had their eyes closed and were continuing in earnest intercession. Fifteen, twenty minutes passed and soon we had been praying for half an hour. I recognised that the 'Spirit of Prayer' had come upon the students, and that I had to let them continue. After about 35 minutes, we gradually came to a stop and there was a strong sense of God's presence in the room. As the Lord moved on me, I gave the following prophecy. Unknown to me one of the students recorded the prophecy. I did not ask for or expect this, and was very surprised when a transcript photocopy of the prophecy was handed to me the following week.

Although several have prophesied along similar lines, I felt the leading of the Lord to include this prophecy in the book.

Prophecy

'There is a stirring coming, there is a stirring coming. In all the nations of the world, I'm calling my people to fervent prayer; for winds have been released, winds of the Spirit. Winds of my angels going forth from the North, and from the South, and the East and from the West. Winds of my power. Winds of my life have been released upon the earth, and the days ahead shall be days of revival. The days ahead shall be days of My power. But in this land, says the Lord, is coming a rumbling, is coming a stirring among my people, and even though it may seem like a cloud the size of a man's hand, says the Lord, in the days that lie ahead, even in the near future, says the Lord, the sky shall become dark with rain clouds of My Glory. Rains of living water will fall upon this land and drench this land and cause life to come forth.

And even in those days, says the Lord, I will use you as my mouthpiece so that you may go boldly and speak the word of life to those around you. And there are coming days ahead of you when you will speak the word to people and they shall come under conviction of sin and they shall burst into tears in front of you as my Spirit reaches down and touches them.

But right now, my people, I call you to fervent prayer. I call you to intercession. I enlist you and I enlist your churches to pray that my Spirit may be poured out upon this land so this land may be drenched with my blessing. So the powers of darkness may be drowned and covered. So that I may have free reign and free rule and freedom to move by my spirit in this land, says the Lord.

So reach out to me; cause your hearts to be full of hope and reach out to me in simple faith, says the Lord, and allow me to do that which I want to do in your land, for I call you and I enlist you to be those who will pray that my glory may come down.'

Chapter 8

Become a Prayer Warrior for the Lord

Earlier on in my ministry I could not understand how God could possibly use someone as ordinary as me. Having grown up as a shy boy, lacking in confidence and self-esteem, I would go to ministers' meetings and look around at the other ministers. They all seemed so relaxed, confident and able to cope that I would shake my head and inwardly say that I was probably the least likely amongst these men to succeed in the ministry – I looked upon them with awe and wished that I could be like some of them.

Several years into the ministry the financial pressures, family pressure, pastoral pressures of church life and the pressure of spiritual warfare, joined together and tempted me very seriously to resign from the pastorship of 'The New Life Christian Centre' in Wembley.

I knew I was called to the ministry and that God had spoken to me very clearly in August 1981 during a time of fasting and prayer. He had shown me that he was going to work in great power in our area with signs and wonders and He told me that even the media would come to find out what was happening. By 1983, nothing of any real significance had happened in the Church. It had grown and a few people had been saved and baptized in the Holy Spirit, but to my knowledge, no one had received healing up to this point – certainly not through my prayers.

By 1983, while under extreme pressure, I decided to go to a *Full Gospel Businessmen's Dinner* in Harrow and then I was definitely going to resign from my Church. The speaker that night was an American preacher, Dan Sneed. He did not know me, but he picked me out of the crowd and told me, through a Word of Knowledge that I was to stay where I was as God had plans that he was working out. He told me more than this but that was the gist of what he said. Well, Dan's word clearly confirmed that resigning was the wrong decision and I knew that I could not possibly disobey God and step out of His perfect will for my life.

Around this time, I began to read several books that told me who I was in Christ. I began to see that I was a child of God and a joint heir with Christ (Romans 8:15, 17). I suddenly began to see afresh that I had authority over the Devil – that I was more than a conqueror (Romans 8:37).

I saw from scripture as I read books on prayer and faith, that God wanted to bless me and lead me into a victorious Christian life (1 Corinthians 15:57–58). As I read these books and met one or two ministers who were a great blessing to me, I began to learn slowly over a period of many months how to have faith – and I began to learn how to pray and engage in spiritual warfare.

Before, I had been passive against the Devil but now I prayed aggressively against evil, driving it away from my life, family, finances and the church. During this time my fellow elders, Doug Williams, Dave Perry and our deacon, Peter Aleksin, were a great support as they too joined me in aggressive prayer.

This was another turning point – to see that many of my problems could be overcome through prayer was a tremendous revelation, not to say – a great relief! Before, I would have sat back and waited for God to do something; Now, I saw that He had provided me with the means by which I could destroy the plans of evil arrayed against me, my family and my ministry.

Certain scriptures came alive to me:

> *Blessed be the Lord, my rock,*
> *who trains my hands for war,*
> *and my fingers for battle;* (Psalm 144:1)

> *'The Lord is my rock, and my fortress, and my deliverer, my God, my rock, in whom I take refuge, my shield and the horn of my salvation, my stronghold and my refuge, my savior; thou savest me from violence.*
>
> *I call upon the Lord, who is worthy to be praised, and I am saved from my enemies.'*
> (2 Samuel 22:2–4)

> *Yea, thou art my lamp, O Lord, and my God lightens my darkness. Yea, by thee I can crush a troop, and by my God I can leap over a wall.*
> (2 Samuel 22:29, 30)

> *He trains my hands for war, so that my arms can bend a bow of bronze. – 38 – I pursued my enemies and destroyed them, and did not turn back until they were consumed. I consumed them; I thrust them through, so that they did not rise; they fell under my*

*feet. For thou didst gird me with strength for the battle; thou didst make my assailants sink under me. ... **43** – I beat them fine as the dust of the earth, I crushed them and stamped them down like the mire of the streets.*   (2 Samuel 22:35–43)

Slowly I began to understand spiritual warfare and put it in perspective. As I began to pray and see myself as God saw me, my whole image of myself began to change: my confidence began to grow and we began to see people healed as we prayed for them.

The Holy Spirit gave me some encouragement during this time. A prominent minister came to my house for lunch and prophesied over me that I would minister across this nation and even to the ends of the earth. Things I had had in my heart for years began to surface and now even looked possible and, praise the Lord, I no longer felt inferior to other ministers.

What you have read above is a condensed version of what happened over many months and years. When we begin to pray and set aside times to pray, the Lord will teach us how to pray. I never like to face a day without the inner strength that prayer gives me.

What is a Warrior?

David fought against Goliath and defeated him (1 Samuel 17). David went on to lead the armies of Israel in victory after victory.

And David went out and was successful wherever Saul sent him; so that Saul set him over the men of war.   (1 Samuel 18:5)

David went from strength to strength and from victory to victory. 1 Samuel 30 is a great study of how David operated. David knew how to pray (verse 8). David knew how to fight and he knew how to win (verses 17–20).

Naturally, David did not always fight alone as he did against Goliath. He had some mighty warriors that fought alongside him.

> *These are the names of the mighty men whom David had: Josheb-basshe-beth a Tah-Chemonite; he was chief of the three;*
> *He wielded his spear against eight hundred whom he slew at one time. And next to him among the three mighty men was Eleazar the son of Dodo, son of Ahohi. He was with David when they defied the Philistines who were gathered there for battle, and the men of Israel withdrew. He rose and struck down the Philistines until his hand was weary, and his hand cleaved to the sword; and the Lord wrought a great victory that day; and the men returned after him only to strip the slain. And next to him was Shammah, the son of Agee the Hararite. The Philistines gathered together at Lehi where there was a plot of ground full of lentils; and the men fled from the Philistines. But he took his stand in the midst of the plot, and defended it, and slew the Philistines; and the Lord wrought a great victory.* (2 Samuel 23:8–12)

Thank God for men like Josheb-basshe-beth who fought alongside David. Joseb-basshe-beth slew eight hundred men all on his own. Now why were these men who fought alongside David called warriors? Why was David called a warrior? What is a warrior?

A warrior is someone who fights and wins – and fights and wins – and fights and wins.

God can put into your heart the spirit of a warrior. God himself is a warrior. In fact he always wins and the Bible tells us that he teaches us how to win as well (1 Corinthians 15:57; 1 John 5:4, 5).

> *The Lord is a man of war;*
> *The Lord is His name.*
>
> (Exodus 15:3; see also: 6, 7)

> *The Lord goes forth like a mighty man,*
> *Like a man of war he stirs up his fury;*
> *He cries out, he shouts aloud,*
> *He shows himself mighty against his foes.*
>
> (Isaiah 42:13)

We saw in an earlier chapter, how in the Old Testament the enemies of God's people were flesh and blood and they had to possess the land by defeating and subduing their enemies. However, since the death and resurrection of our Lord Jesus, salvation has come via the Jews and the Gospel is to be preached to all nations. Now we wrestle not against flesh and blood but against the spiritual kingdom of Satan (Matthew 12:22, 29; Ephesians 6:11, 12).

> *But if it is by the Spirit of God that I cast out demons, then the Kingdom of God has come upon you. Or how can one enter a strong man's house and plunder his goods, unless he first binds the strong man? Then indeed he may plunder his house.*
>
> (Matthew 12:28, 29)

Our war now is in the heavenlies against the powers of darkness and under the leadership of King Jesus, we have the authority and power to defeat Satan and his cohorts using our spiritual weapons.

God wants to enlist you and me in this battle. By His Spirit he will teach us how to fight and win and you too can become a warrior for the Lord.

The way we fight now is with our spiritual weapons. As we employ the Word of God, the Name and the Blood of Jesus learning to pray in the Spirit, we too can learn to live a life of victory. We too can learn to live a life of faith, we too can learn to fight and win in prayer.

We Need to Know Our Rights in God

My people are destroyed for lack of knowledge
(Hosea 4:6)

When we stop reading our Bibles regularly and stop praying, we automatically begin to lose direction in our lives. A prayerless Christian devoid of God's Word cannot be a victorious Christian who is really enjoying his/her walk with the Lord. As we read and study the Bible, we discover our covenant rights as children of God; We discover who we are, what God has made us and what we are meant to be achieving. That is when we can begin to rise up against that liar, deceiver and thief the Devil, and stop him from stealing our joy, provision, healing, protection, peace, victory and all the other things that belong to us when we are walking in fellowship with the Lord.

Many Christians allow the enemy to get away with far too much. Rise up Christian – learn to pray – then go on from there and become a prayer warrior for the Lord.

Victory Prayer Declaration

'According to God's Word I declare that I am a child of God in Covenant relationship with my Heavenly Father. (Romans 8:15, 16)

The Law of the Spirit of life in Christ Jesus has set me free From the Law of sin and death and I am more than a conqueror through him who loves me. (Romans 8:2 & 37)

I am dead to sin and alive to God in Christ and sin no longer controls me. (Romans 6:11 & 22)

I overcome Satan by the blood of Jesus and I testify that I am forgiven and blessed with every spiritual blessing in heavenly places. (Revelation 12:11; Ephesians 1:3)

Jesus is my Healer and my Provider. (Matthew 8:17; Philippians 4:19)

Jesus is my Lord and I will walk in obedience to his Word. (Matthew 4:4)

God supplies all my needs according to his riches in Glory. (Philippians 4:19)

I enjoy God's love and protection and God's angels are around me to deliver me. (Psalm 34:7)

I will serve the Lord this day and all the days of my life and I will bear much fruit with the help of the Holy Spirit my Comforter, Counsellor and my helper.' (John 15:16; John 14:15, 17; Romans 8:26)

Use this declaration daily and boldly, declare who you are and who Christ has made you. As you meditate on the Scriptures above, you will surely receive a fresh revelation of the rights and privileges that are yours in Christ.

Chapter 9

Answered Prayer is God's Will

I had been reaching out to the Lord for several months with a very special request – for my wife Dennise to be able to quit her job and to join me in the work of the ministry. At the time Dennise held a well paid job with a large reputable company and her earnings were a considerable help in making ends meet. I cried out to the Lord week after week in prayer. After several months I began to feel an assurance that this was about to happen. We did all we knew to do and then waited with a sense of expectancy.

One day a young man whom we had known for several years came by our flat and handed me an envelope. I naturally assumed that he had written us a letter and proceeded to open it matter-of-factly. When I opened the letter and viewed the contents I burst into tears as my heart overflowed with thanksgiving to my heavenly father. The letter contained a cheque for £10,000 and was made payable to Dennise. Truly we have a God who answers prayer. As a result of this my wife now works alongside me in the work of the ministry. Her secretarial and administrative skills have proved invaluable in assisting me in my work.

In 1980 I felt the call of God to pastor a church in Wembley. Only in recent years have I felt a wider call on my life to travel to minister and teach. Recently, in addition to ministering outside my fellowship in Wembley, I have had the privilege of ministering in Ghana, Nigeria, Germany and in the USA. Almost everywhere I go, at some point, I feel led to teach on prayer, fasting, spiritual warfare and healing.

I did feel the Lord's leading to write this book, to call all who would hear, into serious prayer. I believe the Lord also gave me the title of this book. Prayer is the message of the hour – it is the call of God across the nations, coming to the body of Christ. As a pastor, I have seen people's lives change, simply as they have learned to pray regularly. Your life will change too as mine has, by continuing in prayer (Colossians 4:2).

In Summary:

Yes, it is so important to pray. In Chapter 1, we saw the Words of Jesus telling us that it was possible to have our prayers answered all the time. Jesus himself said it.

> *If you abide in me, and my words abide in you, **ask whatever you will**, and it shall be done for you.*
> (John 15:7)

As we keep our hearts right with God, as David did, and learn to pray in line with God's promises, we can be successful in prayer.

We observed that God has chosen to work on the

earth largely through the prayers of his people. As covenant children, we can overrule the devil's will and pray for God's kingdom to come and for his will to be done.

Thank God that we can learn to pray, and that we can grow in our faith and win victories as we persist in prayer.

Answered Prayer

Two years ago we needed a new car. The old one was no longer adequate for our needs but we did not have the money to change it. I began to pray earnestly. I would walk along the streets praying for an hour or so, looking at different car showrooms in Wembley.

I reminded God of his promises and began to thank him for a new car. When I first began to pray, I could not imagine how I could possibly get a new car. I tried to ask God for a silver Volvo Estate in good condition at around £7,000. I prayed this way for weeks but I felt weak in my faith.

I knew that Jesus said *'Whatever you ask for in prayer, believe that **you have received it**, and it will be yours'* (Mark 11:24 NIV). I also knew that Jesus meant what he said, and that my need for a car was a genuine need and not just a selfish passion (James 4:3). After a few weeks I just got honest with the Lord and told him that I could not really believe for a silver Volvo Estate costing £7,000 – but I could believe him for a nearly new four door car in good condition both on the inside and the outside.

When I got honest with the Lord about where I really was in my faith, I began to expect my car to show up at any time. A few weeks later a visiting preacher pulled me up before the congregation and said 'your pastor needs a new car – what are you going to do about it?' That day a young man called Errol, a Renault engineer, was visiting our church for the first time. He came up to me afterwards and said the Lord had spoken to him about looking after my car. Shortly after this, the church, with Errol's advice, bought me a nearly new four door car in excellent condition inside and out! It was a smart looking Renault 21 RX with power steering and fuel injection – incidentally the colour was silver. It is the best car we have ever had.

As we pray in line with God's Word and according to our faith, God will answer our prayers.

Chapter 1 was an introduction to the importance of prayer. God invented prayer – he invites us to pray, he teaches us how to pray and he loves to answer our prayers.

In Chapters 2 and 3, we looked at how we really get to know God by spending quality time with Him. Prayer brings intimacy with God and in prayer we are changed as we fellowship with the Lord and hear from him.

We have also seen in Chapters 4 and 5 how we can develop a powerful and effective daily prayer time, and how we can defeat Satan's plans, ploys and strategies through spiritual warfare in prayer.

In Chapter 6, we saw the tremendous benefits released in our lives through prayer and fasting. In Chapter 7, we looked at how we can join with others in corporate prayer to great effect.

In Chapter 8, we examined how we can become a prayer warrior for the Lord.

No other activity we engage in is more important than prayer. Life has many priorities that are important – but let's put prayer at the top of the list and make it our No. 1 priority.

As we fellowship with the Lord and get to know him better and learn to align our prayers with His Word, I believe we will experience that, '**answered prayer is God's will for us**'.